The Battle of Chancellorsville

A Captivating Guide to an Important Battle of the American Civil War

© **Copyright 2020**

All Rights Reserved. No part of this book may be reproduced in any form without permission in writing from the author. Reviewers may quote brief passages in reviews.

Disclaimer: No part of this publication may be reproduced or transmitted in any form or by any means, mechanical or electronic, including photocopying or recording, or by any information storage and retrieval system, or transmitted by email without permission in writing from the publisher.

While all attempts have been made to verify the information provided in this publication, neither the author nor the publisher assumes any responsibility for errors, omissions or contrary interpretations of the subject matter herein.

This book is for entertainment purposes only. The views expressed are those of the author alone, and should not be taken as expert instruction or commands. The reader is responsible for his or her own actions.

Adherence to all applicable laws and regulations, including international, federal, state and local laws governing professional licensing, business practices, advertising and all other aspects of doing business in the US, Canada, UK or any other jurisdiction is the sole responsibility of the purchaser or reader.

Neither the author nor the publisher assumes any responsibility or liability whatsoever on the behalf of the purchaser or reader of these materials. Any perceived slight of any individual or organization is purely unintentional.

Free Bonus from Captivating History (Available for a Limited time)

Hi History Lovers!

Now you have a chance to join our exclusive history list so you can get your first history ebook for free as well as discounts and a potential to get more history books for free! Simply visit the link below to join.

Captivatinghistory.com/ebook

Also, make sure to follow us on Facebook, Twitter and Youtube by searching for Captivating History.

Contents

FREE BONUS FROM CAPTIVATING HISTORY (AVAILABLE FOR A LIMITED TIME) 5
INTRODUCTION 1
CHAPTER 1 - BACKGROUND 3
CHAPTER 2 - NORTH AND SOUTH: COMPARISONS 5
CHAPTER 3 - SUMMARY OF THE BATTLES BEFORE CHANCELLORSVILLE 8
CHAPTER 4 - LEADERS OF MEN 14
CHAPTER 5 - PRELUDE AT FREDERICKSBURG 25
CHAPTER 6 - TWO PLANS, ONE RESULT 34
CHAPTER 7 - JACKSON'S LAST CHARGE 45
CONCLUSION 57
HERE'S ANOTHER BOOK BY CAPTIVATING HISTORY THAT YOU MIGHT BE INTERESTED IN 58

Introduction

Through the centuries, there have been battles that have transcended time. While many battles (some of them quite decisive in their own quiet way) have been assigned a place as a historical footnote, others live with us, sometimes centuries or even millennia after they took place.

The Stand of the 300 at Thermopylae, Alexander's defeat of the Persians at Gaugamela, Caesar's victory over the Gauls at Alesia, the revolutionary victories of Napoleon before his defeat at Waterloo (itself a symbol of utter defeat), the American victory at Yorktown to end the Revolutionary War, Gettysburg, the Battle of the Somme in World War I, Pearl Harbor, Stalingrad, the Bulge, the Tet Offensive...and so many more.

For military scholars, armchair historians, and "buffs" of the American Civil War, there is one other battle that should be included on that list, for it was a masterpiece of military planning and execution, though, in the end, its impact was less decisive at the time than it might have been on the officers and men who studied it afterward.

The Battle of Chancellorsville took place in 1863. One hundred fifty-seven years later, what Robert E. Lee and Thomas J. "Stonewall" Jackson did on that battlefield in Virginia is still being taught at the

United States Military Academy, also known as West Point, and other military schools around the world. This battle, more than any other in the Civil War, cemented these two Southern military leaders as legends, as bold and innovative battlefield commanders. In fact, the battle has come to be called "Lee's Perfect Battle." Jackson, however, would not live to enjoy the laurels of their victory, but that we will discuss in great detail toward the end of this volume.

With their victories at Chancellorsville and at Fredericksburg, which took place immediately afterward, the Confederate Army was able to mount its invasion of the North, which ultimately took them to a small town in Pennsylvania named Gettysburg—but that is a battle for another time.

Chapter 1 – Background

Let's be clear—the American Civil War was fought over slavery. Some may argue that the conflict was fought over "states' rights," and there can be a logical point made for that. However, the one "right" the South was fighting to keep the most was slavery.

Since its inception, the United States had been wrestling with itself over the issue of slavery. How could a nation founded on the principle that states "All men are created equal" allow the enslavement of others? People today still wrestle with that. They needn't do so. For most white people in the South and a good many in the North, "Africans" (the polite name that many in the community were referred to as) were not *people.*

By the beginning of the Civil War, Africans had been in bondage in North America for about two and a half centuries. They were captured or bought (from other Africans or Arab slave traders) in Africa and then brought to the Western Hemisphere. They were also bred into slavery. Children and their parents were torn from each other, just like chattel animals. With the ratification of the US Constitution in 1787, slaves were labeled as "three-fifths" of a person for tax, census, and political reasons.

In the years between the establishment of the United States and the start of the Civil War in 1861, the government and the people of America wrestled with the question of slavery. By 1852, with the publication of *Uncle Tom's Cabin* by Harriet Beecher Stowe, many in the North were pushing for the abolition of slavery in the entire country or, at the very least, the prevention of new "slave states" being established.

In the South, where the economy was based on agriculture, the sentiments to limit or eliminate their virtually cost-free source of labor didn't fall on deaf ears—in fact, it enraged the people. The North, which was much more populous than the South, was also far richer and was seen by many (especially by the ruling classes in the southern part of the country) as pushy and power-hungry. To them, it seemed as if the men in the North were trying to gain more power by eventually freeing the slaves. The liberated black Americans would naturally side with the Northerners politically, and the Southern way of life, which was seen, at least by those on top, as "genteel and aristocratic," would be made extinct.

A war was fought in the 1850s in Kansas and Missouri, two territories vying for statehood, and this war became a literal battleground for the question over the expansion of slavery. By the end of 1860, virtually everyone in the United States believed that a civil war was inevitable, and on December 20th of that year, South Carolina became the first state to secede from the Union.

It's also interesting to note (and some Southern apologists use this for their "states' rights" argument) that a number of states in which slavery was legal remained in the Union. These were Maryland, Delaware, Kentucky, and Missouri (though the latter two had a significant number of men fighting for the South).

Chapter 2 – North and South: Comparisons

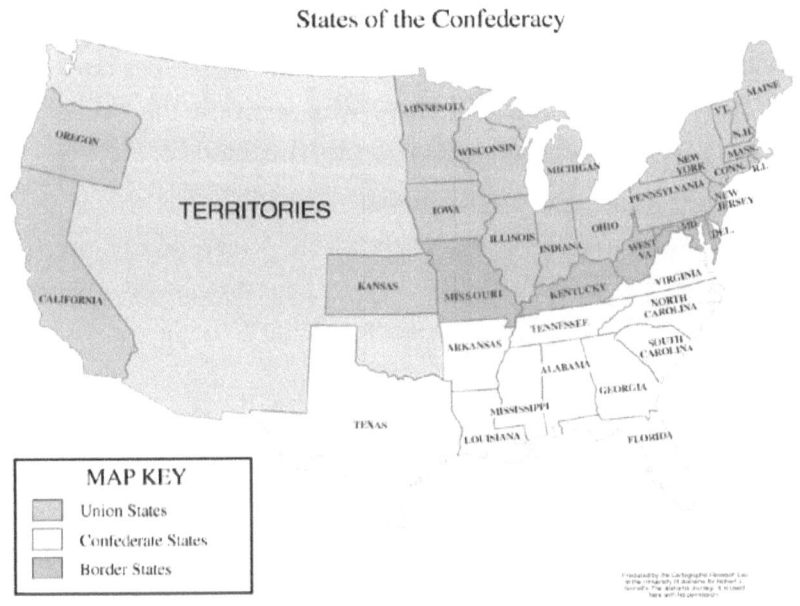

States of the Confederacy

Within a short period, the eleven states that eventually made up the Confederacy seceded from the Union. Too many in South, this had been a long time coming, but when it came, the South was woefully unprepared for what was to come.

In the South, there was a popular misconception that the Northerners would not fight to keep the South in the Union, or at the very least, they would not fight for long, especially once they had their noses bloodied. For reasons that could form their own book, many of the men of the South, whether they were from the upper classes with aristocratic bearing and ideas of martial "honor" or from the tough farmers and backwoodsmen, felt that the men of the North were soft, that they were either city boys that had no experience fighting or farmers whose rich soil almost grew crops on its own with little hard work involved.

This preconceived notion also meant that the South's material unsteadiness was either overlooked or downplayed by many. The South was overwhelmingly agricultural, with its few industries located mainly in the cities on or near the coast, such as Richmond, Charleston, and Atlanta. This also included their limited war-making capacity. The Confederates did not have the arms that they needed when the war broke out, and that's why some of the South's initial moves were to seize federal arsenals and army bases in the South.

However, as it would become increasingly clear, the South was unable to move troops as effectively as the North due to the lack of railroads. By the second half of the war, the North was able to shift troops rapidly from one part of the country to the other as their strategies demanded.

Lastly, the South's greatest weakness was its lack of manpower. Twenty-two million people lived in the North, while nine million lived in the South. Of these nine million people, over three million were slaves. This large number of the slave population also meant that a sizable portion of the white Southern male population had to remain out of uniform, as slave uprisings were a constant worry during the war. Amazingly, however, in the first year of the war, before the North became very serious about the conflict, the Confederate forces in the field almost equaled that of the Union.

Despite all of these problems, the South did have some advantages during the war. First and foremost, they did not have to attack the North. The defenders almost always have an advantage in modern wars (and some historians believe the US Civil War to be the first "modern" war)—the South could fortify and defend. They did not have to waste their manpower in an invasion of the North, which is why some still question Robert E. Lee's decision to do so in the summer of 1863, but that's a story for another time.

The Confederacy also had a distinct advantage in leadership. While there certainly were bad Southern generals, at the beginning of the conflict, the scales of leadership were decidedly tipped in the Southerners' favor. While the following is a generalization, many of the leading Southern families expected their sons to serve at least some time in the military, as it was the "manly" thing to do. A disproportionately large segment of the United States Army's officer corps was from the South, and many of those, such as Lee and Jackson, had combat and leadership experience in the Mexican-American War in the 1840s.

At the beginning of the war, many, but not all, of the Northern generals were political appointees or had been desk-bound for a long time. It was not until about the mid-point of the war that the lower and mid-level officers of the North, who were young and capable with combat experience under their belts, moved into top leadership positions.

But those leaders were not present at the Battle of Chancellorsville in the spring of 1863.

Chapter 3 – Summary of the Battles before Chancellorsville

The Battle of Chancellorsville came at almost the mid-point of the Civil War, and though they certainly had setbacks, the Confederate Army did unexpectedly well—unexpectedly well to the men in Washington, DC, in 1861, that is. As with most wars, both sides believed their armies would sweep forward and end the war quickly. If you ever hear a general or politician saying, "The war will be over by Christmas," you can almost be assured that it will *not*. History bears that out.

Very generally speaking, the men of the Union looked at their foes as outnumbered and outdated, at least in regards to their aristocratic thinking and ideas of "honor." They also thought of the average Southern soldier as a barefoot backwoodsman who was not all that smart. They were right about the first one, though—the South was certainly outnumbered. However, the Southern ideas of honor and their so-called aristocratic thinking were overblown, and these ideas actually sometimes played to the South's benefit, as the men in the South followed natural leaders and oftentimes appointed them on their own. All too often in the North, officers were often political appointees, desk-bound officers who hadn't seen a battlefield in years or ever, or men who simply bought their way into a general's uniform.

One of the more stereotypical views the North of the South was the aforementioned backward "backwoodsmen." Think about that for a moment. Yes, a significant portion of the Confederate Army was poor, uneducated, and illiterate. Some left-leaning historians have said, with some accuracy, that the poor whites of the South had more in common with the slaves than they did with the leading families who owned most of the land and the fabulous estates like the fictional Tara in *Gone with the Wind.*

What did that mean for the Confederate Army, though? Foot soldiers don't need to be smart or even literate, especially in the 1860s. What it meant to them was an army full of men who were used to hard work and hunting for their supper. Or, to put it more bluntly, the men of the South could shoot, and they could fight.

Of course, the Southerners made the same mistakes when it came to their view of the Northern soldiers. Not all of the Northern officers had paid their way into their positions, and many of the soldiers of the North also had to hunt to supplement their diets. As for the "city-boys" of New York, Chicago, Philadelphia, and Boston, it would be fair to say that they knew how to use their fists and didn't mind a fight.

Many with only a passing knowledge of the war sometimes make the mistake of thinking that the conflict was only the series of the large and more famous battles we read about in history books or see on television. However, if fighting did not take place every day, it came close. The battles of the Civil War are too long to expand on for our purposes here, so we will try to keep the battles before the Battle of Chancellorsville brief. Suffice it to say that within a short period of time, people on both sides realized this was likely going to be a long and costly war.

In 1861, the Civil War began, and it started with the southern siege of Fort Sumter in the harbor of Charleston, South Carolina. As most know, after a prolonged cannonade, the Union outpost surrendered, and secessionists throughout the South cheered wildly.

The first land battle of the Civil War was not actually the First Battle of Bull Run, as most believe, but an action at Philippi, in what was then western Virginia (West Virginia became a separate state during the war). Though relatively small in size and today considered to be a skirmish rather than a battle, the Union victory convinced many in the North that the war would be short.

The first large-scale land battle of the war was named after two geographical features. In the North, the battle was and is still known as the First Battle of Bull Run, named after the small river that runs through part of the battlefield. Southerners know the battle as the First Battle of Manassas for the name of the town/road junction in the area. The battlefield was only 25 miles from Washington, DC, and it took place on July 21st, 1861. Famously, Washingtonian journalists, party-goers, and socialites gathered picnic baskets and went by carriage to the site of the battle, knowing full well that a battle was shaping up in the area (at this stage in the war, the troop movements were barely hidden). The observers expected an old-fashioned, well-organized Napoleonic battle (at least that's what they had chosen to believe) and a decisive Union victory.

Twenty thousand Southerners met thirty-five thousand Union troops at Bull Run, and after hours of fighting off many poorly led and costly Union attacks, the rebels counterattacked, outflanking the Union right and creating a panic in the Union lines. Terrified Union soldiers, some horribly wounded, ran or were carried away screaming through the terrified onlookers, who realized too late that war is not a spectator sport.

Despite their victory, the rebels were too few and too disorganized to push onto Washington, DC, but the battle showed that the Southerners were able to defeat the Union Army in battle and with fifteen thousand fewer men.

During the war, the rebels and their leaders developed a well-earned reputation for dashing and audacious attacks, but it was in the defense at Bull Run/Manassas that one of the most famous men of the Civil War earned his nom de guerre. Thomas Jonathan Jackson, a West Point graduate, Mexican-American War veteran, and an artillery instructor at the Virginia Military Institute, held back repeated Union attacks during the battle. Southern General Barnard Bee Jr. rallied his men by pointing out Jackson "standing like a stone wall."

The war also took place at sea, and on March 14th, 1862, the Union ironclad USS *Monitor* met the CSS *Virginia* at Hampton Roads, Virginia, in the world's first battle between armored ships. Most of the world knows this battle as *Monitor* v. *Merrimack*, but the latter had been renamed after iron plating had essentially changed the ship completely.

Between March and June 1862, "Stonewall" Jackson led a brilliant campaign in Virginia's Shenandoah Valley, a campaign that is still considered to be a masterpiece of mobile warfare. This campaign kept the Union off-balance and kept a vital supply area of theirs in chaos.

In the early summer of 1862, Union General George McClellan, outfitted with a powerful army, attempted to outflank the Confederates in Virginia in order to capture the capital of Richmond. Believing himself to be outnumbered (he most definitely was not), McClellan moved slowly and cautiously after assuring President Abraham Lincoln he would capture the Southern capital in a rapid and overpowering dash up the peninsula between the James and York Rivers south of the city. During the battle, Confederate General Joseph E. Johnston was wounded, and Robert E. Lee took command of the Confederate Army of Northern Virginia.

This led to what is known as the Seven Days' Battles, which included the bloody Battle of Malvern Hill. The result was a Confederate victory and an embarrassing loss for the Union Army and its commander.

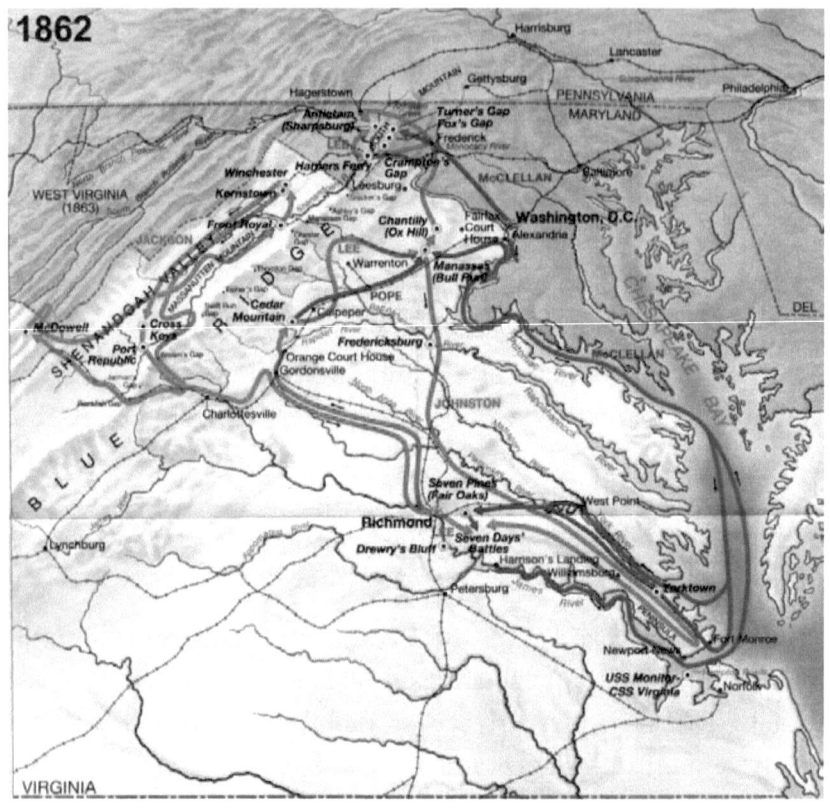
Illustration 1: The Campaigns in the East, 1862

In August, the South won the Second Battle of Bull Run, also known as the Second Battle of Manassas, which opened the way to Lee's first invasion of the Northern territory. However, this push into the North ended with a bloody stalemate at Antietam (known as the Battle of Sharpsburg in the South), which Lincoln astutely and politically called a victory since the Union troops remained on the field.

During all of this, battles were raging in the west, along the Mississippi River and in Tennessee, such as those notable conflicts at Shiloh and Stone's River/Murfreesboro, whose casualties, like those at Antietam, shocked the nation. Also, in the west, a formerly washed-up officer named Ulysses S. Grant was given one last chance at command, and he began a brilliant campaign to take control of the

Mississippi. He was joined there by another "washed-up" officer, William Tecumseh Sherman. The two would later work hand in hand to defeat the rebellion once and for all.

In December of 1862, the two sides concentrated large numbers of troops near Fredericksburg, Virginia. In a series of poorly planned, poorly executed, and poorly led attacks, the Union troops charged virtually unassailable Southern positions, leading to a slaughter of Northern men and the firing of yet another Union commander. The war went on, but the two sides remained engaged with or nearby each other in the Fredericksburg area for months, looking for a weakness or a mistake that would let them win a decisive victory or seize the enemy's capital. After all, Richmond and Washington, DC, lay just over one hundred miles apart.

Though a number of battles took place in the east during the winter and early spring of 1862/63, mostly on the coasts of the Carolinas and Georgia, it was not until the late spring that the large decisive battles began again. And it was here that the Battle of Chancellorsville would take place, starting on the last day of April and ending during the first week of May 1863.

Chapter 4 – Leaders of Men

Robert E. Lee

Any chapter on the leaders in the Battle of Chancellorsville has to begin with Robert E. Lee. As was mentioned earlier, Chancellorsville is considered Lee's "masterpiece," and it is still considered one of the most influential battles in history, at least from the point of view of the military arts.

Robert E. Lee came from the American aristocracy, or at least as near to it as was possible in what was supposed to be an equal society. Lee's grandfather, Henry Lee II, had been an influential politician in the days before and during the American Revolutionary War. His father, known to history as "Light-Horse Harry" Lee, was an aide to George Washington during the Revolution and a skilled cavalry officer. Robert E. Lee himself was related to George Washington both by marriage and by blood—he married Mary Custis, the great-granddaughter of Martha Washington and George's step-great-granddaughter. He was also distantly related to the general himself, as they were third cousins twice removed. In Virginia, the Lee family was almost like royalty, and much was expected of their sons. However, like royalty, Lee's father was extremely bad with money, and Lee grew up in a comparatively deprived environment compared to his peers.

Illustration 2: Lee in the Corps of Engineers, 1838

Lee was unable to afford a university education, so he sought an appointment to West Point. In 1829, he graduated second in his class, attained the highest rank of the cadets, and won the support of all around him—he had a quiet charm, dignified Southern manners, and was a natural leader of men.

He toiled away in the Corps of Engineers for years. At the time, the engineers were considered the elite of the army, tasked with helping to build the new nation and construct, among other things, its coastal forts. But that meant that advancement was slow since the competition was stiff. It was not until the Mexican-American War (1846-1848) that Lee was able to show his brilliance on the battlefield that he later became a legend for. Though performing exceedingly well throughout the campaign in Mexico, Lee is most famous in the Mexican-American War for the dangerous scouting trip he took through Mexican lines to find a weakness and allow the Americans to win the Battle of Veracruz in 1847. Robert E. Lee and Ulysses S. Grant actually knew each other from their time they worked in concert in Mexico.

After the Mexican-American War, Lee held a variety of posts, including a position as the superintendent of West Point for three years from 1852 to 1855. Lee was on leave at his home in Arlington, Virginia, when John Brown's anti-slavery revolt began at Harper's Ferry in 1859; Lee was assigned to put it down, which he did swiftly. Much has been made of Lee's views of slavery, and extremists on both sides hold very simple views. One side says he was a cruel slave master, and there were certainly times when he could be, but on the other hand, he also freed some of his slaves and helped others move to Liberia, a fairly new nation in Africa that had been founded by ex-slaves.

Much of Robert E. Lee is an enigma, though. For example, he was quiet and the symbol of self-control, but those closest to him knew that he had a boiling temper. His views on slavery were somewhat at odds with each other as well. He believed that whites were superior to blacks; however, he also thought slavery was evil but that it was a necessary one, and he participated in it himself. He thought that "someday" it would die of its own accord, without political interference. Lee, like other Southerners, had a belief that slavery was decreed by God, and when God saw fit to remove it, He would. Lee did not believe that the Northerners could understand the predicament of the South and its "peculiar institution," as many called it.

Famously, when the Civil War broke out, Lee was asked to take the command of the Union Army, he but turned it down, and after much painful deliberation, he instead elected to fight for his home state, Virginia. He became Virginia's commanding officer, but it was a desk job, which mainly consisted of advising Confederate President Jefferson Davis. (Note: before the Civil War, most Americans referred to themselves from their state first and as Americans second, if at all. This sentiment held true in the North, too, but was more ingrained in the South.)

Initially, Lee was assigned a variety of busywork. He gathered supplies, helped to secure troops, and provided equipment where it was needed most. He worked at this for the first eleven months of the war. In the spring of 1862, he worked with Stonewall Jackson for the first time, helping him to plan his famous Shenandoah Valley Campaign. In May 1862, Confederate General Joseph E. Johnston was wounded fighting Union Major General George McClellan on the James River peninsula, and so, Lee took command of the Army of Northern Virginia.

Lee took a group of heterogeneous men and whipped them into an army, and within a short time, after having fought a series of battles against McClellan that kept the Union general flummoxed and off-balance, he managed to form the Army of Northern Virginia into one of the most famous fighting forces in American history.

Stonewall Jackson

Thomas Jonathan "Stonewall" Jackson was born in 1824 in Clarksburg, Virginia, which is now West Virginia. Like Lee, he grew up poor, but he had no "name" or illustrious figures to follow in the steps of. His father and sister died early, followed later by his mother. Jackson was raised by relatives, moving from house to house as necessary.

Also, like Lee, Jackson sought an appointment to West Point, but he only got in when the student chosen before him decided to quit after one day. Jackson had a time of it at the academy. He was older than most of the others and was also from a much more modest background. Though he attended West Point decades after Napoleon Bonaparte went to the École Militaire in France, one could find similarities between the two, though not in stature. Jackson was poor and relatively uneducated. Napoleon, though from an upper-class family, was a "foreigner" from Corsica with little formal education at the time. Both were teased for it, as well as for their other differences. But in both cases, this bullying drove them on. Jackson graduated near the top of his class in 1846, the year the Mexican-American War began.

Jackson, like Lee and Grant, fought with distinction in Mexico, and he met Lee on a number of occasions, though Jackson was an artillery officer, and Lee was in the Corps of Engineers. When the war ended, Jackson was welcomed home as a hero and had risen to the rank of major from lieutenant. He served in New York and Florida, then retired from the military in 1851 when he was offered a professorship at the Virginia Military Institute (VMI).

Illustration 3: Jackson as a young officer

In addition to teaching artillery tactics, Jackson also taught a variety of science classes, as well as philosophy. Unfortunately, Jackson's stay at the VMI, which lasted until the dawn of the Civil War, was much like his student career at West Point: He was a highly unpopular teacher. He was demanding, surprisingly unoriginal, and he was "peculiar," as the students and other teachers there likely put it. Today, we might just say "weird."

His quirks later endeared him to his men and to history, but this was before he was victorious on the battlefield. He sometimes taught with one arm up in the air, believing that one arm was longer than the other and that this might help even them out. He later did this on horseback during the war, and he likely took a bullet because of it. Jackson also believed that eating pepper weakened his left leg and avoided using the spice. A myth saying that Jackson sucked on lemons came after a post-war book was published on the man. This tale may have started because Jackson was an abstemious eater but a voracious eater of fruit.

Jackson married in 1853, but his wife Elinor died in childbirth the next year. He remarried three years later, but this marriage was also marked by tragedy. Though his wife lived into old age, their daughter died within one month of being born. Jackson and his second wife, Mary Anna Jackson, had another daughter in 1862, but she sadly never knew her father.

Jackson was there when John Brown was hanged, as he was representing the VMI. When the Civil War broke out, Jackson hoped Virginia would remain in the Union, but when that did not happen, he, like Lee, decided his loyalty lay with his home state and not the distant federal government and the North.

Jackson's exploits at Bull Run and in the Shenandoah Valley have already been recited, albeit briefly. Suffice it to say that by the end of the Shenandoah Campaign, Jackson had established a reputation as one of the most brilliant tactical officers of the war, one heralded in the South and respected, feared, and hated in the North.

Illustration 4: Jackson before the Chancellorsville Campaign

Other Confederate Generals

Also present at Chancellorsville was a list of some of the most well-known generals of the war. There was the already famous cavalry commander James Ewell Brown Stuart, better known as Jeb, who had been running Union troops ragged since the start of the war, as well as Jubal Early, who fought throughout the war and fled the country after the war ended. Early would later return and deliver speeches around the country, ennobling the cause of the South and helping give birth to the "noble underdog" sentiment that still lives on today. Besides these two distinguished men, there was also Lafayette McLaws, who led a stout defense at Fredericksburg and repeated charges at Gettysburg; A.P. Hill, who was one of Jackson's favorite officers and mentioned in his last words—it is notable to mention that Hill was killed just seven days before the end of the war; Richard Anderson, who, like many of the South's leading generals, had fought in Mexico in the 1840s; Raleigh Colston, who was born in France and whose adopted mother was of French nobility, and Robert E. Rodes, who was the first of Lee's coterie of general officers not to have been at

West Point and who was chosen by Jackson to lead the decisive move at Chancellorsville. Lastly, General Ambrose Wright led a division of Georgians and distinguished himself enough to rise from colonel to brigadier general in a short time. After the war, he actually took part in US national politics for a short time.

Fightin' Joe Hooker

Facing Lee and Jackson at Chancellorsville was Joseph "Fightin' Joe" Hooker. A more unfortunate nickname would be tough to find. Today, Hooker is known primarily as the man Lee defeated in his "greatest battle," but prior to Chancellorsville, Hooker had distinguished himself well in some of the war's early major battles: Williamsburg, Antietam, and Fredericksburg.

The nickname was a mistake, a typo of sorts by a traveling journalist, but it stuck. Hooker had a pugnacious personality, and it seemed to fit. He was likely an alcoholic and may have shown more bluster than he actually had. His headquarters was famous for its drunken and raucous parties, and it's likely, but not assured, that the word "hooker," meaning "prostitute," came from these parties, as the girls there were of "easy virtue."

Illustration 5: "Fightin' Joe

Hooker was a Massachusetts man who had fought in the Seminole Wars in Florida and held staff positions for future president Zachary Taylor and future general of the army Winfield Scott. In those positions, he likely came into contact with Lee, who served on Scott's staff in Mexico for a time. He also likely knew Grant and of Jackson. Hooker was not just a paper pusher—in Mexico, he was cited for gallantry in three battles.

In 1853, Hooker was involved in testifying against his former commander (and national hero) Scott in a trial concerning another officer. This likely damaged his chances for promotion at the time, and he increased his reputation for women and drink that he had started in Mexico. Eventually, he quit the army and moved to Sonoma County, California, trying his hand at farming and running unsuccessfully for the state legislature. Finding farming boring, he joined the state militia in 1859 and was on duty there when the Civil War began in 1861.

Hooker applied to rejoin the federal army but was rejected. On his own dime, he traveled to Washington to lobby those in power for a position. He was among those who went to view the First Battle of Bull Run, and he wrote a stinging detailed criticism of the leadership and conduct of the Union's failure. This article got him the commission he wanted, and Hooker was made a brigadier general and worked to reorganize the army under the newly appointed General George McClellan (who, despite having a reputation as a cautious commander today, is and was known as a great organizer).

During the Peninsula Campaign, Hooker proved himself and tried to push McClellan into a more aggressive policy, albeit unsuccessfully.

At Antietam, which is considered to be the Union's first major victory by many, Hooker engaged with Stonewall Jackson's unit for much of that bloody day. He led from the front and eventually had to be taken off the field under protest when he was wounded in the foot. After Antietam, Hooker was again critical of McClellan, who many were seeing as fainthearted and not willing to press the fight.

After the disastrous defeat at Fredericksburg, Hooker was named commander of the Union Army of the Potomac on January 26th, 1863, and set out to develop a plan to destroy the Confederate Army in Virginia and take Richmond. Perfecting his plans in May, he said, "I have the finest army on the planet. I have the finest army the sun ever shone on...If the enemy does not run, God help them. May God have mercy on General Lee, for I will have none."

Other Union Generals

In his planning to defeat Lee in the Chancellorsville area, Hooker was joined by several notable generals, including George Stoneman, who is noted to history as the leader of the last Union cavalry raid of the war in 1865, and George Meade, who would replace Hooker and go on to defeat Lee at Gettysburg. Dan Sickles also joined up; he made the term "(temporary) insanity defense" part of the American legal lexicon when he was acquitted for the murder of his wife's lover before the war. Incidentally, that lover was the son of Francis Scott Key, the author of the "Star-Spangled Banner," the national anthem of the United States. O.O. Howard, who became the namesake of Howard University; Henry Slocum, who was one of the youngest major generals of the war and who saw action at most of the more famous battles in the east; Darius Couch, who was later responsible for critically delaying Lee in his approach toward Gettysburg; and John Reynolds, who was a respected commander that was later killed on the first day of Gettysburg, were also among the prominent names that helped Hooker plan and fight in his campaign.

Chapter 5 – Prelude at Fredericksburg

Fightin' Joe Hooker's plan to defeat Robert E. Lee's Army of Northern Virginia was a good one. In actuality, it was sort of the mirror opposite of the one Lee was developing.

If you've read about the Civil War in books with pictures, or have seen pictures of the men of the period on the internet, you might notice an interesting phenomenon. Like today's "social media" where photographic trends and poses catch on fast and spread like wildfire, the Civil War era had its own fashionable trends. Perhaps the most recognizable was what we might call the "Napoleon pose."

The French general and emperor was famous for being depicted in paintings (photography did not exist at the time) standing erect in a dignified posture with one hand tucked inside the opposite side of his uniform's closure. Such a pose can be found in the painting by his favorite painter, Jacques-Louis David, below.

Napoleon revolutionized warfare, stressing the importance of audacity and mobility, and he frequently defeated armies many times his size. In the US, his military skill was revered, and his tactics and strategies were taught not only at West Point but at academies around the country. Military men wanted to be like him. Hence, portraits like the one below, this time of Union General George McClellan, whose nickname was "Little Napoleon."

The point of this little example is to stress how much influence Napoleon Bonaparte had even some forty years after his death. And while we don't know for sure if Robert E. Lee and Stonewall Jackson, or even Joseph Hooker, were thinking of Napoleon as they planned for their spring campaign in 1863, his ghost was there without doubt, for as the generals sat down to their map tables, they planned maneuvers that easily could have been planned by the French master of war.

Let's begin with Joe Hooker. Hooker came to the command of the Army of the Potomac with the dismissal of General Ambrose Burnside, who had led the Union Army at the Battle of Fredericksburg in December 1862. Many historians consider Fredericksburg to be part of the Chancellorsville Campaign; though they took place months apart, they were fought in the same area for the same goals.

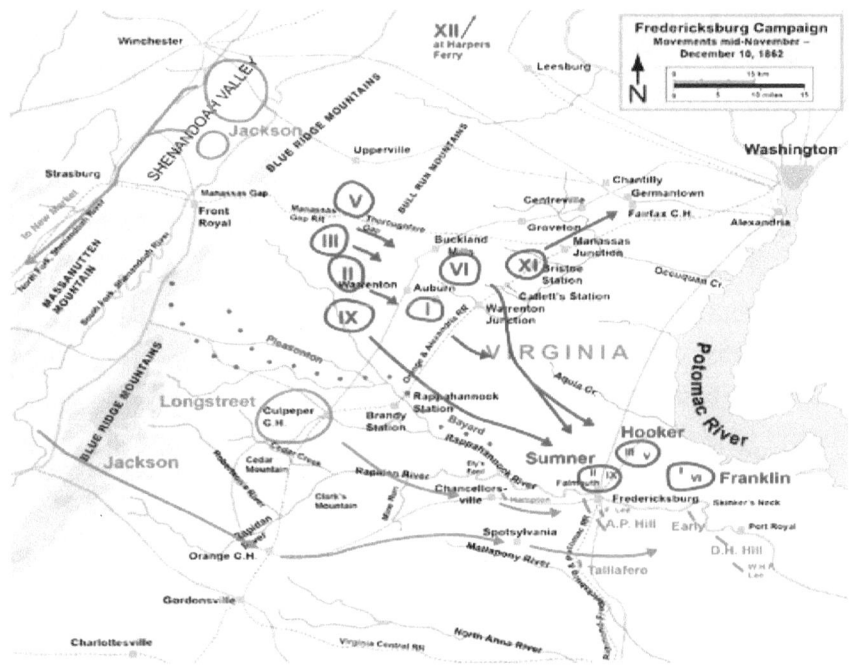

Illustration 6: This public domain map shows the movements of both armies leading to the battles in the Fredericksburg/Chancellorsville area of Virginia

The Battle of Fredericksburg marked a new low point in the Union war effort, which, with some few exceptions, had already experienced many low points. Burnside's armies faced Lee's across the important Rappahannock River in Virginia, only about sixty miles north from Richmond.

Virginia's rivers vary in size, from the small creek-like Bull Run to the wide Potomac. The Rappahannock was a medium-sized river. It was 184 miles long, and at Fredericksburg, it was deep enough and wide enough to need bridges to cross. The website of Fredericksburg today gives this warning about the river: *Although the river is very beautiful and seems calm and serene in most places, it can be very dangerous for those who enter it unprepared and without a life jacket.*

Just outside and west of the town itself, on the northern part of the Union lines, was a canal and a wide ditch that had to be crossed during any attack. In the center and south of the Union front was the Rappahannock. Before the two armies faced each other, the rebels destroyed the bridges leading from the town of Fredericksburg into the populated farmlands beyond, which was where they took up exceedingly strong positions that were helped by the topography—beyond the riverbank were slopes that the Union Army would have to scale before reaching the Southern lines. Though the battle took place along about a two-mile front, the most famous point along the Confederate lines was called Marye's Heights (pronounced "Marie's"), located at the northern end of the line.

On the cold, gray morning of December 13th, 1862, the Union began its assault on the Confederate lines outside Fredericksburg. Burnside's aides and fellow generals had lodged vociferous protests against the assault, as they were sure it was going to be virtual suicide. They were right, but Burnside, whether in the back or the forefront of his mind, decided that he was going to be the opposite of the fired George McClellan (whose cautious nature had gotten him dismissed) and attack the Southerners with "dash and elan," two of the favorite words of the time. His best course of action would have been caution—waiting out the weather and then moving his army in an attempt to get a better position. It was certainly unlikely, his aides argued, that the rebels were going to attack across the river themselves—they were outnumbered, and the Union occupied the stout buildings of the town (which they looted without mercy). In one of those buildings, Chatham Mansion, Lee had courted his wife decades earlier. In 1863, the house was Burnside's headquarters, and Lee could see it from his lines atop the heights opposite the town.

In warfare, especially in the 1860s, it was almost law that an attacker had to have at least a two to one advantage in men for a successful assault. Burnside didn't have that, though he came close. The Union forces numbered about 114,000 men, and the South had about 72,000 to 73,000. There was no way the Southerners were going to launch an attack on Burnside, and his best choice would have been to pick another place to fight.

But he didn't, and while Fredericksburg was not the bloodiest battle of the war, it might have been the most tragic of a war full of tragedy. In Ken Burn's award-winning documentary, *The Civil War*, a southern officer is quoted telling General James Longstreet (who would not be present at Chancellorsville) that when the North attacked his four-deep lines of riflemen at Marye's Heights, "General, a chicken could not live in that field when we open on it." He was right.

The Union men came in rows—thousands of them. When they got within cannon range, the Confederates opened up on them with cannonballs and canister shot (think giant shotguns at almost point-blank range). The wounds and screams were horrendous, but the Union men marched on. When they closed to within just yards of the Confederate riflemen, the rebels opened up with volley after volley from four ranks of men. The Northerners fell by the hundreds, but they still pressed on. In the back ranks of the rebels, as they reloaded and as their officers directed their fire, they actually cheered the bravery of the Union soldiers coming at them. They also raged against the stupidity of the Union officers that had ordered the assault. It wasn't a fight. As one of the Southern soldiers said afterward, "It was plain murder." The Union troops charged, fell back, and charged again *fourteen times.* Paraphrasing the preeminent Civil War historian Shelby Foote, "To this day, most people believe that the

Southerners possessed the most dash and bravery, but I know of no greater example of bravery in the war than that of the Union troops fighting at Fredericksburg."

Though Marye's Heights is the most (in)famous part of the Battle of Fredericksburg, it was not the only part. To the south of Marye's Heights, another Union assault was supposed to take place in conjunction with the assault about a mile northward, but it was delayed due to the late arrival of the elements that made up the pontoon bridges the Union intended to use to cross the Rappahannock south of the town.

As you can see from the picture above, which was taken after the battle, the rebels could easily have blown the parts of this bridge to pieces as the Union brought them down to the river, but they didn't. They knew exactly how strong their positions were, and they were sure that no matter how many "bluejackets" (as the Union soldiers were sometimes called) Burnside threw over the bridge, they wouldn't make a dent in the Southern positions, so Lee, Jackson, and the other Southern commanders decided to let the Union "come on across." In actuality, they would pile atop each other in wave upon wave, crowding the area before the slopes where the Southerners were waiting. Eighty-two years later, men from both the North and the South, fighting together this time, would pile onto the beaches of Iwo Jima in much the same way, and they were slaughtered in staggering numbers when the Japanese opened up on the overcrowded beaches.

Illustration 7: A contemporary painting of one of the Unioncharges at Fredericksburg

One of the men making the attempt to dislodge the rebels above Fredericksburg was a professor at Bowdoin College in Maine. Joshua Lawrence Chamberlain, who would lead his men to glory at Gettysburg just a few months later, was part of the charge up the slopes. At the end of the day, he, like many other men, waited for nightfall to attempt to retreat. Before they did so, they lay among the dead and wounded, listening to men screaming, crying for their wives and mothers, and begging for their comrades to put them out of their misery. He used two dead bodies as a shield from the rifle fire that slowly petered out as night fell, using the lapels of one dead man's frock coat as a cover to try to sleep.

During the late afternoon and late evening, some rebel atop the heights would shout down to the Union men, "Jesus Christ! Shoot the poor bastard! We won't shoot!" They had enough of murder during the battle.

The Union sustained some 13,000 casualties compared to the South's 5,000. Many of those wounded later died or were removed from the war effort due to the nature of their wounds.

Oftentimes, people who are first learning about the American Revolution or the Civil War (or other contemporary wars in Europe) wonder: why did they march directly in groups right into enemy rifle and cannon fire? It's actually easy to answer. For centuries before the Civil War, the firearms of the time were notoriously inaccurate. For the best results, troops banded together, aiming in the direction of a group of men doing the same. Obviously, whoever was the most steadfast, loaded quicker, and developed new tactics (such as one rank firing while another loaded, and so on) got the most results. However, by the time of the Civil War, virtually all front-line troops were using rifles as opposed to muskets. Rifles are called that because the spiral in their inner barrel is called "rifling," which makes them much more accurate—and deadly. It's an unfortunate military axiom that nations always prepare for the *last* war because they don't anticipate a future one. And so, the men of the Civil War, even until the end, marched at each other row on row, which is one of the reasons this war was the deadliest in American history.

The next morning, General Burnside, likely feeling both guilt and anger over what had passed the day before, wanted to personally lead one more charge on Marye's Heights. His officers, though, talked him out of it. In an age before psychology, they probably knew enough about human nature to know that Burnside was trying to commit suicide—with glory. The only problem with that was that hundreds of more men would die.

Burnside sent a messenger under a white flag to General Lee, asking for a truce to remove the dead and wounded from the field, which Lee granted. Later that day, the Union Army moved out of Fredericksburg to the opposite side of the Rappahannock. Entering the town of Fredericksburg, Stonewall Jackson and his staff saw firsthand the looting and damage the Northern troops had done to the quaint Southern town. One of Jackson's aides asked him, "General, how we goin' to put an end to all this kind of thing?" and Jackson said, "Kill them. Kill them all."

On the night of December 14th, a rare show of the aurora borealis was seen over parts of Virginia, including Fredericksburg. The Confederates took it as a sign that God was pleased with their victory. The men of the Union probably thought the opposite.

Though Burnside was able to improve his reputation in the battles in Tennessee under Grant, he later was partially blamed for a colossal failure at the Battle of Petersburg and resigned just before the end of the war.

Chapter 6 – Two Plans, One Result

The armies of the North and the South remained in the Fredericksburg area after the battle. The risk to either side was grave. The Army of Northern Virginia held a strong position, as we have seen. There was no reason to give the enemy a chance to regain momentum and push toward Richmond. Should the Union forces retreat, they could possibly give Lee a chance to approach or assault Washington, DC—and any step back toward the Union capital might have grave political implications.

Though there were dissident voices in the South, they were much less numerous and far quieter than those in the North, where Abraham Lincoln had to deal with opposition to his leadership from Congress, his Cabinet, and from within the disparate ranks of his Republican Party. In other words, any retreat back toward Washington could jeopardize Lincoln's presidency.

Following the disaster at Fredericksburg, Burnside attempted another flanking move to get at Richmond in January, known to history as the "Mud March." This, too, was a failure, and desertions, which were already rife, increased. He also attempted to dismiss many of the staff officers of his army, which he did not have the authority to do. Already having to listen to grumblings from the sidelined

McClellan (who, strangely enough, retained some popularity—enough to seek the presidency in 1864), Lincoln was not about to cede more control of the Army of the Potomac to Burnside. Rebuffed, Burnside resigned and was transferred west, as mentioned above.

Joe Hooker had made good arguments in his analysis of the First Battle of Bull Run and McClellan's abortive Peninsula Campaign. He showed confidence and an urge to fight. Some had doubts because of his reputation as a drinker, and Lincoln had gotten word of Hooker's off-the-cuff comment about the country "needing a dictator." He appointed Hooker anyway, saying to him, "I have heard, in such way as to believe it, of your recently saying that both the Army and the Government needed a Dictator. Of course it was not for this, but in spite of it, that I have given you the command. Only those generals who gain success can set up dictators. What I now ask of you is military success, and I will risk the dictatorship."

Hooker set about doing a number of things right away. Though today "Fightin' Joe" is sort of an object of ridicule for the disaster that was to follow, a number of the changes he installed were an improvement over the way things had been done with Burnside. Firstly, he fired a number of Burnside's officers and replaced them with men of his choosing.

Secondly, he reorganized the way the Army of the Potomac was structured. Burnside had organized the army into what he called "grand divisions." Readers familiar with World War II will know that a "corps" usually consists of somewhere between two and five divisions. In Burnside's system, the corps was subordinated to the "grand division" and proved, because the roots of the system were based on large units, to be unwieldy and slow to move in battle.

Third, Hooker instilled a new sense of discipline and pride in his men. Food and sanitary/medical conditions were improved, officers were given more rigorous training, and the quartermaster corps was reorganized and subject to greater oversight because of widespread corruption (which you might know if you've seen the movie *Glory*).

Hooker also made greater and better use of his cavalry to scout enemy positions, increased the use of observation balloons, and employed a greater number of scouts and spies than previous commanders. By the time of the Battle of Chancellorsville, which began in earnest in late April, Hooker could congratulate himself on a job well done because the army after Fredericksburg was a mess.

Hooker's Plan

Originally, Hooker had hoped that a bold drive of virtually all of his cavalry (some 10,000 men) around Lee's flanks toward Richmond and into Lee's supply lines would force Lee to retreat from the Fredericksburg/Chancellorsville area to protect the Confederate capital. When Lee retreated, Hooker would pursue him "with all vigor" as Lee moved toward Richmond, hopefully being able to bring his greater force to bear on a retreating and disorganized enemy. It was a good idea—on paper. And if the weather was good—which it wasn't. On April 13th, 1863, General Stoneman moved out, and it soon started to rain hard, turning the few roads, tracks, and fields into mud that made the use of cavalry impossible in any useful way. Within two days, he had barely covered a handful of miles and was forced to turn back. On hearing this, Abraham Lincoln, like a sports fan whose team had started the season with promise year after year and gone nowhere, told his aides, "I fear it is a failure already."

General Hooker was forced to draw up new plans after the failure of Stoneman's "raid." He and his staff came up with a plan that was in many ways bolder than anything the Union Army in the east had planned before. His intention was to hold Lee in place in the area of Fredericksburg with a sizable portion of his force, then move the rest of his army in a "double envelopment" of Lee, whose army was in the area between the small town of Chancellorsville and the Spotsylvania Court House (which had its own bloody battle in 1864).

Chancellorsville is about ten miles from Fredericksburg, and while today the countryside features the same rolling hills and pastoral countryside, in 1862/3, it was much more wooded, and only a few dirt tracks ran through it, making observation much more difficult than it would be today (all things being equal). But even today, Chancellorsville is a small town that is kind of in the middle of nowhere in a crowded state. The battlefield is the only reason most people have heard of it. In the 1860s, this was truly a rough territory, and it made maneuvering and deployment, at least for those unfamiliar with it, exceedingly difficult.

One section of Hooker's army would move northward from its base at Falmouth, just to the north of Fredericksburg, on the northern side of the Rappahannock River. This section would first swing north then west toward Rappahannock Station at Kelly's Ford and cross the river there. This branch of Hooker's forces would consist of the men under Generals Meade, Howard, and Slocum, with General Sickles in reserve to the north of the main movement of the troops. Their job was to circle around Lee's western flank and strike him there, trapping his forces between Chancellorsville and Fredericksburg and destroying the Army of Northern Virginia for good.

At Falmouth and Fredericksburg, Generals Sedgwick (who was wounded at Antietam, took no action in Fredericksburg, and was later killed in action at the Battle of Spotsylvania in May 1864) and Reynolds would hold the mass of Confederate forces, feigning attacks but not "pressing them home" unless a real opportunity presented itself. In other words, they were to do just enough to worry the rebels and keep them in place, but they were not to expend their troops on another frontal assault, like what had happened in December. Hooker messaged Sedgwick, "It is not known, of course, what effect the advance will have upon the enemy, and the general commanding directs that you observe [Lee's] movements with the utmost vigilance, and should he expose a weak point, attack him in full-force and destroy him." When Hooker got word that his northern units were in position, the forces at Fredericksburg would do their bit.

Illustration 8: Hooker's plan at Chancellorsville

It was a great plan, if it could be carried out in the manner in which it was designed. Though it is an overused phrase today, boxer Mike Tyson's quote about plans bears repeating here: "Everybody's got a plan until they get punched in the mouth." That quote could not be more appropriate for the situation at Chancellorsville in 1863.

As you can see, Southern General Thomas "Stonewall" Jackson was in overall command of the rebel troops in the Fredericksburg area. Jubal Early commanded the troops in and around Fredericksburg itself. Under him were Generals A.P Hill, Lafayette McLaws, and Raleigh Colston. Lee's headquarters was to the rear and to the west of this, with Generals Anderson and Wright protecting the western flank to the southeast of Chancellorsville.

As for Robert E. Lee, he listened while his aides and generals debated as to what General Hooker was up to. They knew something was afoot, for there was a great deal of movement reported and intelligence had come in about movement to the west, but there was nothing certain. On April 30th, Lee had his binoculars out and, along with his staff, was observing the Union positions. His men were debating on whether Hooker was going to come straight at them from the southeast or from the north. Lee lowered his glasses and said, "The main attack will come from above," meaning the north. He was exactly right.

For his part, Lee was concerned that he would have to deal with a force to his north and then worry consequently or concurrently about Hooker moving to his south between Lee's army and Richmond, depending on how Hooker's attack went. Lee determined that he would face the Union Army he believed was moving northward to flank him first, then file the armies of Jackson at Fredericksburg westward in a staggered manner, hopefully making the Union men in the town believe a sizable force still remained fixed there.

Jubal Early was to remain in place in Fredericksburg and the area around it, and he was given a brigade from McLaws in addition. Still, the rebels in Fredericksburg were drastically outnumbered by the Northern troops, but they had a strong position, and perhaps the Union men would not realize what was happening, especially since the blood-soaked heights would hide the Southern movement to the west.

Lee also believed that Hooker would not attack in just one place, but he did not have enough men to defend everywhere. An old military dictum goes something like this: "Defend everywhere, lose everywhere." Lee would have about 45,000 men to move west to hopefully catch Hooker's force moving southeast from the west, which was still far fewer than his enemy, and 10,000 in the lines at Fredericksburg.

What Lee did went against military dictum, and much has been written about it since. What that means is that logic dictates that you shouldn't divide your force in the face of the enemy when he is stronger than you. However, if Hooker was doing what Lee believed he was, remaining in one place would only get him surrounded by a superior enemy, and retreating toward Richmond was both militarily and politically risky. In the mind of this writer, Lee did the only thing he could have done—but that is written with 20/20 hindsight.

All this time, Lee was receiving reports from his dashing cavalry commander, Jeb Stuart, who was saying that the Union forces were on the move to the northeast of Chancellorsville and were beginning to turn southeastward. Stuart had taken prisoners from three Union corps, and while these soldiers did not know the extent of Hooker's plans, just the fact that three corps were represented meant that a sizable army was approaching Lee from the west, just as he had anticipated. He told Stuart to keep scouting but to "anchor his forces at Chancellorsville."

On the night of May 30th, Lee ordered his generals to begin their movement out of Fredericksburg. General Richard Anderson was already digging trench lines about four miles to the east of Chancellorsville, and Lee ordered McLaws to move his men beginning at midnight to the area around Anderson's positions. Lee instructed Jubal Early, who was left with just one division along the entire front at Fredericksburg, to "keep up a bristling pretense of strength and aggressive intentions."

Jackson gave his orders to McLaws and Anderson at 11 a.m. By 11:20, the Battle of Chancellorsville had begun.

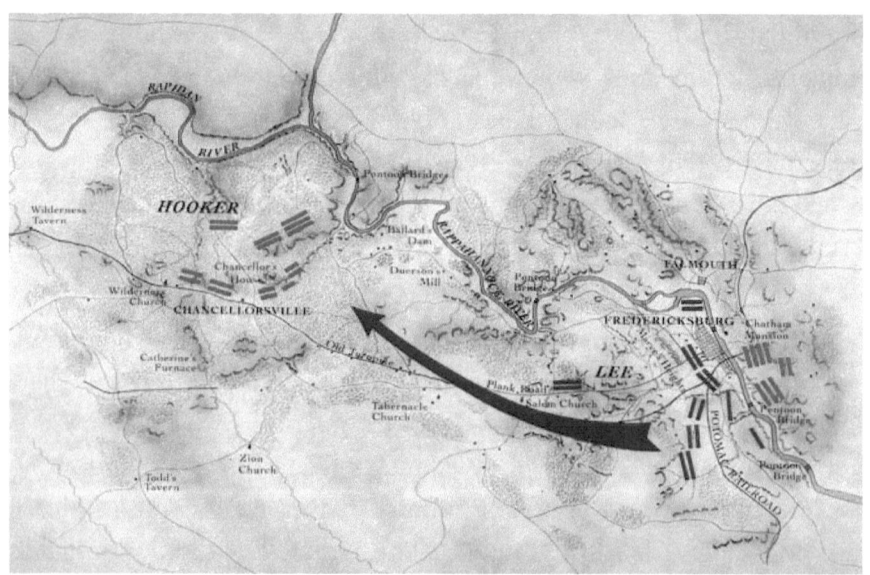

Illustration 9: In this map from PBS, you can see the general movements and dispositions of troops on the first day. The large red arrow includes all Confederate columns moving west to meet Hooker.

Hooker was not idle either. He had been issuing orders and coordinating as much as possible with his commanders in the field. Looking at the map above, you can see the "Tabernacle Church" below the red arrow marking Lee/Jackson's movement. At the tip of the arrow is where the forces of the North and the South first met. Hooker had given orders to Generals Slocum and Meade to march from Chancellorsville to find and defeat the rebels. He had also reaffirmed his orders to the men in Fredericksburg to make a demonstration to hold the Southerners in place. Hooker was not aware that most of the rebel troops had abandoned their Fredericksburg positions and were heading right at him.

General Meade, dubbed a "mean old goggle-eyed snapping turtle" by someone now unknown to history, and later the victor at Gettysburg, was to move with General Slocum in the direction of the Tabernacle Church with Generals Couch, Sickles, and Howard following behind. Meade was to lead his troops along the Orange Turnpike, to the north of the Plank Road, which was designated for Slocum's troops. Near the church, the two roads came together, and hopefully, the Union columns would meet there to strike the rebels in unison. It was a good plan. On paper, or in the mind, most plans seem good—that's why people begin them. But remembering Mike Tyson's quote, not all plans bear fruit.

Meade's and Slocum's troops were supposed to keep in contact with one another, which was seemingly easily done since the turnpike and the road were less than a mile apart at their farthest, about halfway between their starting point and the Tabernacle Church. However, the entire area from just east of Chancellorsville far to the west was called the "Wilderness."

And the Wilderness was just that, the North American version of a jungle. Trees were close together, and in between were masses of brush and bramble for miles on end. Somehow or another, these men, who had seen this area for much of the past year and a half at least, believed that messages could be speedily relayed through the Wilderness. They must have believed that the distance, which was less than a mile, could be covered quickly. Anyone who had tried to get through heavily forested and thorny terrain with no roads and no recognizable landmarks will know that a single mile can seem like ten, and instead of the twenty or so minutes it would take a man walking at three miles per hour, it might take an hour or more. Add the necessity for being vigilant and quiet, and more time is added to cover that distance. Meanwhile, the column you are looking for is moving, and the heavily wooded rolling hills have an additional feature as they sometimes mask sound or make it seem like it's coming from an entirely different direction. For an attacker, this can be a benefit, but when you are trying to find someone, it is not.

So, as one might surmise now, Meade's and Slocum's columns lost contact with one another. Making things more difficult, one of Meade's divisions was farther north on the River Road, its aim being to launch a left hook into the Southern right or rear flank, whichever presented itself.

As Meade's main force on the Orange Turnpike crested a hill and came into view of the eastern edge of the Wilderness, they came under fire from Confederate skirmishers. One of Meade's commanders, General George Sykes, marched down the turnpike and was the first to encounter the mass of Confederate troops under McLaws, who opened fire upon Sykes' men with all they had. Soon the rebels began moving toward Sykes' troops and began to swing left and right to envelope the Union men. Sykes sent word rearward that he was in trouble and began to retreat back down the turnpike in an organized fashion.

One of the rear columns, that of General Couch, was marching down the turnpike as planned, led by General Winfield Scott Hancock, another man who would go down in history at Gettysburg.

Couch ordered Hancock to move up quickly to aid Sykes, but as Hancock got his men in ready order and Couch prepared to follow, word came from Hooker: "Withdraw both divisions to Chancellorsville." Both Hancock and Couch were confused. The battle had barely begun, and that by only part of the larger Union Army, and the Union men had the higher ground and more cover. Yet Hooker was ordering a withdrawal.

Couch sent word back to Hooker that the situation was advantageous and that the battle had not even truly begun. Couch could hear gunfire coming from his right, which meant that the men of Slocum's column were engaged with the enemy as well, but to him, they seemed to be holding their ground, which they were. To their left, Couch and Hancock could not hear anything, which meant that General Meade was likely not engaged yet, which was not a bad thing, for the ideal situation would be for Meade to strike the Confederate right or rear. Within thirty minutes, they all got the same order from Hooker: Retreat to Chancellorsville.

Couch and his aides debated disobeying the order, and his chief engineer rode back to Hooker's headquarters to explain to Fightin' Joe the benefits of staying in place. While he was gone, however, Couch's training kicked in, and he began to organize his men to follow orders, as he had learned at West Point, and to engage in a fighting retreat. Sykes fell back first, then Hancock. Two regiments were left to follow behind as a rearguard once the other formations had organized themselves and begun to move. As that was happening, it seems that Sykes' engineer, General Gouverneur K. Warren (who would be a hero later on at Gettysburg), had had an effect on Hooker, who sent back another order: "Hold until 5 o'clock." By this point, it's likely that Couch and Hancock were getting the same feeling they had experienced before—an inept commander. Couch grabbed a messenger. "Tell General Hooker he is too late. The enemy are already on my right and rear. I am in full retreat." It was likely the process of trying to obey Hooker's orders that had moved the Union troops into a much less advantageous position. The fighting ability of the Union foot soldiers was up to the task, but once again, their high command was not.

To Couch's right (to the south), a similar situation was occurring. General Slocum had received similar orders and was being pursued by Confederate General Anderson. Additionally, in the north, General Meade had received the same orders that all of the other Union leaders had. He was even more mystified and disgusted. Meade had not even engaged the enemy yet, and he was in a position to cut south and perhaps appear at the enemy's rear. Meade was heard to remark the following about Hooker and the good positions that he was ordering his men to give up: "If he thinks he can't hold the top of a hill, how does he expect to hold the bottom of it?" Still, orders were orders. It was two o'clock in the afternoon. The battle was only three hours old, and the Union was already in retreat. Things were not going well, and they were going to get far, far worse.

Chapter 7 – Jackson's Last Charge

During the evening before, Lee had met Jackson to discuss his plans and give final orders. This was to be the last meeting of the two, and this meeting, today located and memorialized with a small stone marker in a fork in the road, has entered American, especially Southern, mythology. Paintings have been done, plays written, and movies made that included this scene. Here is one painting below, along with a picture of the marker.

Illustration 10: The meeting lasted much of the night. According to tradition, Lee and Jackson sat on cracker barrels during part of the conference. Afterward, the generals got some sleep. The next morning, James Power Smith of Jackson's staff noted that Jackson had a fever. Painting and text courtesy National Park Service

Jackson himself was ordered to move out at daybreak but chose to do so at 3 a.m., before sunrise. When Jackson arrived to meet with McLaws and Anderson, whose men were digging in about four miles to the southeast of Chancellorsville, Jackson ordered them to stop and to follow him—he was going to attack at the first opportunity.

Lee's orders to Jackson were vague. That wasn't a mistake. Lee trusted Jackson enough to know that the man knew what he was doing. Jackson and his men had fought some forty battles in the last eight months, from the Shenandoah Valley to the heart of Virginia, most of them victoriously. To Jackson, he gave orders to proceed to where McLaws and Anderson were digging in. Digging in was not Stonewall Jackson's style, though. He knew there was a time and a place for it, such as at Fredericksburg, but this wasn't Fredericksburg. This was what was literally known as the "Wilderness" of Virginia—perfect for hiding movement and to outflank and surprise his enemies by using the terrain. Jackson's orders were "to proceed" to the Chancellorsville area. He had done that. But he wasn't ordered to stop there. In addition to McLaws' and Anderson's men, his own three divisions were coming up from Chancellorsville and would be there before mid-morning at the latest.

Jackson was sure the enemy was ahead, either at Chancellorsville proper (which at the time was less a "ville" than just one structure) or very close by. His men had seen Union soldiers in the woods that fled when they were spotted. Jackson was sure Hooker's main force was very, very close.

The Germans, considered to be the masters of military planning for centuries, have a term for a military leader who has a knack for moving his troops at just the right time and in just the right way. That term is "fingerspitzengefühl." The literal translation is "finger tips feeling," but that doesn't convey the true meaning. Definitions.net has a great definition: "It describes a great situational awareness, and the ability to respond most appropriately and tactfully." However it is defined, Jackson had it in spades. And Lee probably had more.

At that evening meeting, Lee had told Jackson of an audacious idea, which was Jackson's favorite kind. Earlier in this work, we mentioned the idea that military logic dictated that a weaker force should never divide its forces in the face of an enemy. When Lee moved part of his army out of Fredericksburg and its approximately 30,000 soldiers, leaving just 10,000 men, he did just that. No one questioned it—they knew Lee. They also knew that the man would discuss his plans and listen to ideas, incorporating them if necessary, but once his orders were given, he expected them to be followed without hesitation.

So, Lee and Jackson decided that they would divide their forces yet again. Jackson would take his 26,000 men approximately fourteen miles to the west, then quickly turn east down the western branch of the Orange Turnpike directly at Hooker's right flank, which was commanded by General Howard. Lee and his corps commanders would remain in the southeast near the old smelting center of Catherine's Furnace. Lee would have 17,000 men with him. These 33,000 men would be trying to outmaneuver and surprise Hooker and his 73,000 troops.

Aside from the disadvantage in numbers, Lee and Jackson were faced with broken communications; any messages between the two would have to take a wide route, as the enemy would be between the two of them, known as "exterior lines" to military tacticians. Hooker possessed the "interior lines," where communication would be easier.

However, Jackson would have surprise on his side. He would also be attacking the end of the Union lines with a broad front of his men. In old naval warfare, this type of maneuver would be called "crossing the T." The illustration below shows this tactic.

Illustration 11: Crossing the T

As you can see, the ships in the top line would be able to bear the guns from six ships on the first enemy ship while the ships of the vertical formation would only be able to employ the guns on the first ship. Now, take a look at the map below, showing the situation at Chancellorsville on the late afternoon/evening of May 2nd, 1863. On the far left, you can see Jackson's divisions "crossing the T" of the right of the Union lines.

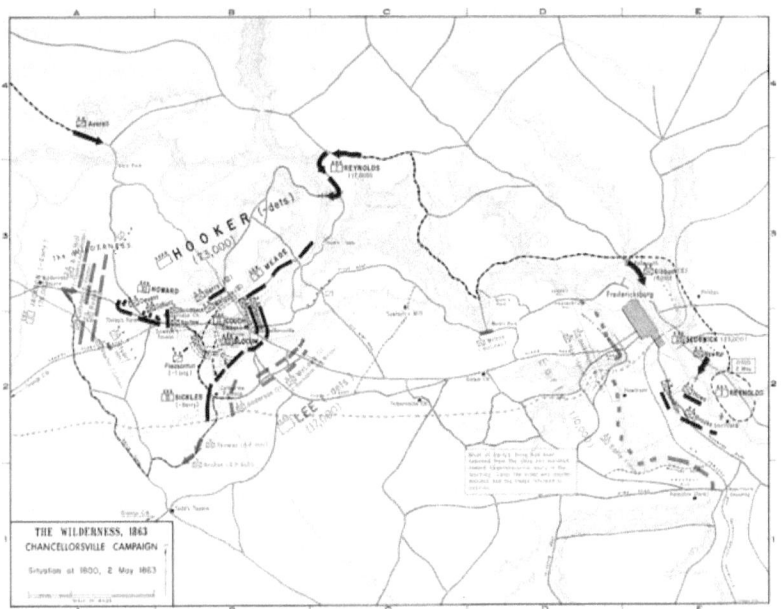

In the Union camp during the evening/night of May 1st and 2nd, there was discussion and much dejection about what had happened during the day. Why had Hooker ordered his men to retreat when they held such an advantage? Historian Shelby Foote, whose three-volume history of the Civil War (whose first volume was published in 1958 and has been revised over time) is still considered to be the definitive history of the conflict, believed Hooker's cautiousness had a number of reasons behind it. First, Lincoln, knowing Hooker, had warned him to "beware of rashness." Foote also put forward the idea that Hooker, a heavy drinker who had "sworn off" liquor for the battle, was feeling the effects of an alcoholic in withdrawal. He didn't face any severe pain, but without his emotional crutch, Hooker might have found himself second- and third-guessing himself. Other historians agree this might have been a factor. Third, Hooker might have wanted to succeed where others had failed, but his fear of failure may have outweighed his drive to succeed.

Aside from these somewhat uncertain but likely accurate assertions about Hooker's personality, he was also receiving information from his scouts, prisoners of war, and even spies he had within the

Southern ranks. All of this information suggested that Lee was planning a strong attack with *all* of his forces on the center of Hooker's line, which was anchored on the Orange Turnpike on both sides of Chancellorsville and south to the area of Catherine's Furnace. If Lee did intend to do this, Hooker was more than ready for him: he had interior lines, his men had been digging entrenchments all night, and he had more men and guns. Hooker was hoping that Lee would repeat what Ambrose Burnside had done at Fredericksburg—a frontal assault on a very strong fortified position.

The problem was, Lee wasn't that stupid. Nothing in what he or Jackson had done up to that time suggested that he intended to attack Hooker's strongest point. Oddly enough, two months later, at Gettysburg, that's exactly what Lee did—and he regretted it to the day he died.

Meanwhile, while he was waiting on Jackson, Lee planned on keeping the Union men engaged. Throughout the day, the two sides engaged each other in a bloody fight, but Lee ordered his officers not to press the attack. He wanted Hooker to believe he would, which would keep the Union commanders' eyes fixed on him and not Jackson, whose forces peeled off for their fourteen-mile march at daybreak.

Jackson could not take a straight route to his destination. At one point, he would have to dogleg south in order to remain undercover. Jackson's attack would also benefit from three other things that he likely was not aware of in moving out. One, the men holding the Union right were made up mostly of recent immigrants from Germany, many of whom did not speak English well, if at all. This meant that their commanders' orders took much longer than they should have to be understood and obeyed. Two, their commanders, General Howard and Brigadier General Francis C. Barlow, were both highly unpopular martinets—high on discipline, low on skill. And thirdly, most of the regiments on the Union right had either never been in a winning battle or even seen action.

Hooker got reports that there was movement to his right, and he ordered a detachment to pursue. He thought, but was not positive, that Jackson's movement (Hooker did not know it was Jackson, however) was the beginning of a retreat back toward Richmond. In case it wasn't, he wanted to stay in contact with the enemy column, but Hooker was prevented in this by hard fighting at the end of Jackson's column by the 23rd Georgia Regiment. Jackson's main column was also screened on its northern flank by Jeb Stuart's cavalry, who moved between it and the Union, preventing the enemy from getting closer.

At 5:30 p.m., Jackson's men had reached their jumping-off place, screened by the woods and located along the Orange Turnpike and Ely Ford's Road to the north. Jackson's divisions were three-deep, with General Rodes leading, followed by Colston's and A.P. Hill's divisions.

The Union troops, at the conjunction of Ely Ford's Road and the Orange Turnpike, were commanded by General Charles Devens, who had his forces formed to anchor the far-right of the Union line. Despite all that was to follow, Devens personally acquitted himself well, being seriously wounded during the battle yet refusing to be taken from the field until the fighting was done. Here he is, pictured below, in the characteristic Napoleonic posture.

Illustration 12: Devens during the war

Jackson's force covered just under two miles north to south abreast the two roads. Its final position before the attack was around one thousand yards from the Union forces, the first of which possessed only two cannons, which was a mistake in the extreme, for they were the end of Hooker's line. Should they be "rolled up," Jackson would hit each successive Northern unit in the flank, repeatedly "crossing the T." These men were also settling down to dinner, thinking another day had gone by (for them) without battle or injury.

At 5:15, Jackson sidled up to General Rodes on his horse Little Sorrel (who is actually stuffed and on display at the Virginia Military Institute today) and asked, "Are you ready, General Rodes?" Rodes replied, "Yes sir," and Jackson told him, "You can go forward then." All of Jackson's men had been ordered not to stop *for anything*. If they needed help, they were to send runners back but to keep advancing.

The Union men in the clearing near the conjunction of the two roads didn't hear a thing—at first. But they did see something. A lot of things, in fact, Dozens of deer running toward them, through their camp, in panic. Rabbits by the number, darting this way and that. Flocks of birds flying out of the trees overhead.

Suddenly, they were confronted with thousands upon thousands of rebels wearing their grey or (actually more common) butternut colored uniforms while letting loose the infamous "rebel yell," which by all accounts was a chilling series of high pitched yips and howls, all of which could (and often did) send chills up the spines of the Union men. Jackson and his aides remained in the rear as long as he could stand it, but Jackson soon joined his advancing, screaming men, ordering them to "Press on! Press on!" as he went.

Illustration 13: "Press Forward Men." Jackson at Chancellorsville. Painting by Bradley Schmehl

Panic ensued. What few men that could turned and fired their weapons, then ran, if they weren't gunned down or bayoneted to death. The two cannons were fired, then abandoned—the Southerners turned them around and took them for themselves. As they advanced, the Southern ranks spread out, allowing Colston's and Hill's men to enter the fray, sending three Union divisions into a panic and driving them back toward the small settlement of Fairview. Hundreds of men were killed, many were grievously wounded, and many were taken prisoner. The Confederates suffered greatly as well, for some Union troops, especially among the veteran troops closer to the Union center, turned around and fought hard.

The battlefield was in complete darkness by 7:30. Though Jackson didn't want to, the darkness forced him to halt his attack. This also allowed the fleeing Union troops to reorganize and form lines in a U-shape around Chancellorsville. The men under Lee to the south had been fighting hard during the afternoon, pressing Hooker into a smaller and smaller area around the "town."

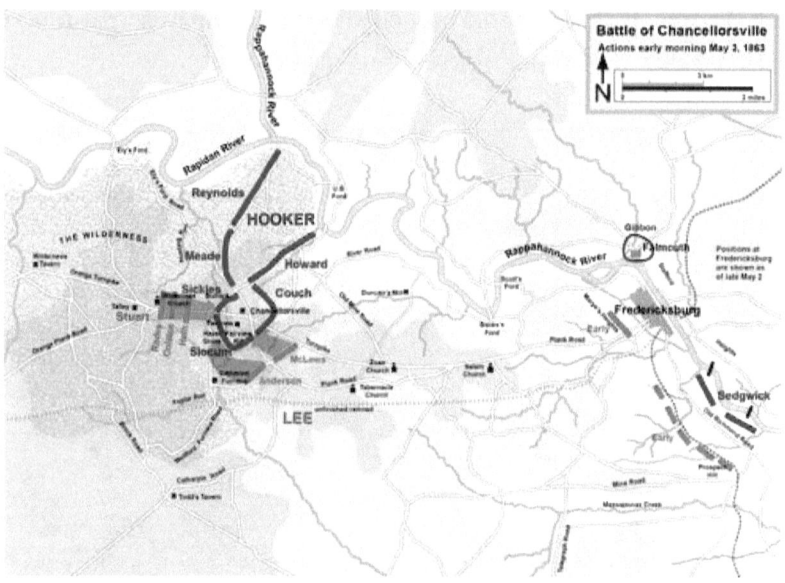

Illustration 14: The situation on the morning of May 3rd

There would be more fighting the next day, and for a time, Chancellorsville would have the dubious distinction of being the costliest battle of the costliest war in US history. For the South, however, one of these casualties greatly tempered the joy they felt at their seeming victory. On the night of May 2nd, while reconnoitering his lines, Jackson and his men surprised a unit of North Carolinians, who had shortly before been engaged in a hard fight with men from Pennsylvania, including hand-to-hand combat. They fired on Jackson and his officers, who yelled, "Cease fire! Cease fire!" But the Carolinian commander believed it to be a Union ruse and ordered his whole unit to open fire, which they did. Among others, Jackson was hit, and badly. He took two bullets in his left arm and one in his right hand.

Entire volumes have been devoted to Jackson's last days. Suffice it to say that his left arm was amputated almost immediately upon reaching his own field hospital. He awoke not long after and gave his command to A.P. Hill, but Hill was also wounded. Command devolved to Jeb Stuart, who had never led infantry forces before; however, he performed very well the next day. On May 10th, despite appearing to improve for a time, Jackson died of pneumonia, which he may have had before the battle, but which his wounds had exacerbated. In his last hours, Jackson came in and out of lucidity, sometimes ordering men to do this or that. At other moments, he understood his doctors telling him that his time was short. "It is the Lord's Day," Jackson said. "My wish is fulfilled. I have always wanted to die on a Sunday." His very last words were, "Let us cross over the river, and rest under the shade of the trees." Upon hearing of Jackson's wounds, Lee said, "I would rather have lost my right arm."

Both sides had taken tremendous casualties, but there was more fighting to be done on May 3rd. Some of it took place at Fredericksburg, where Union General Sedgwick launched multiple attacks on Jubal Early's positions, realizing they were more thinly held than previously thought. Eventually, Early carried out an orderly retreat after another bloody battle at Fredericksburg, moving west to join Lee in his positions around three sides of the Union lines.

The fighting near Chancellorsville began at 5:30 a.m. with the Confederate cannons outnumbering the Union guns (for the only time in the war in Virginia) and pounding them mercilessly. The Union men acquitted themselves well, but since they were all but surrounded, and having their morale shattered by the events of the day before, they retreated at 9:30 to begin crossing the Rappahannock. During this fighting, Hooker was wounded when a cannonball struck his headquarters. A concussion knocked him out for over an hour. When he came to, he refused to be taken off the field, but for the rest of the day and into the Union retreat, Hooker was a beaten, timid man.

The rebel units, which had been pressing from west and east since Jackson's charge, now united in a solid front, but they, too, were weary of fighting. As Lee moved into the mass of troops in Chancellorsville, wild cheering went up, tempered only by the knowledge that Jackson had been seriously wounded.

For the next two days, fighting continued. By May 5th, the Union forces had been pushed back over the Rappahannock, and the rebels had pushed them away from Fredericksburg. In Washington, DC, Abraham Lincoln heard the news. "My God! My God! What will the people say?"

The Union losses at Chancellorsville were just over 17,000 killed, wounded, or missing. The Confederate totals were almost as bad: nearly 13,000 men killed, wounded, or missing. Though the South had won a great military and moral victory, the losses were tremendous, and the South had far fewer men. A few more "victories" like this, and the South might lose—or more hopefully from the South's point of view, the Union would lose heart. Robert E. Lee had a plan for making them do just that.

Conclusion

After the battle, Hooker was replaced by George Meade. A.P. Hill eventually recovered and took over Jackson's command.

Chancellorsville was Lee's crowning achievement of the war. He had defeated, in a shocking manner, a force over twice his size, and his reputation in both the South and the North grew. Some, in both parts of the country, started to feel as if he could not be beaten. Lee never succumbed to that idea, except perhaps briefly on the third day at Gettysburg, but that was two months away.

Chancellorsville had rocked the Union Army and dealt a blow to the Union cause. Politically, it weakened Lincoln and emboldened his enemies in Washington, many of whom wanted to come to terms with the South and end the war.

For Lee, the movement of the Army of the Potomac back toward Washington in relative disarray meant that the way was open for his planned invasion of the North, which he hoped would force the North to come to terms, but that is a story for another volume in this series.

Here's another book by Captivating History that you might be interested in

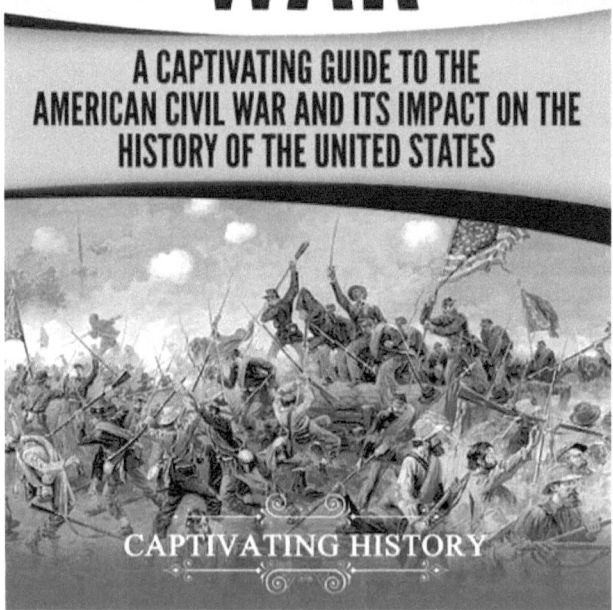

References

Foote, Shelby. *THE CIVIL WAR, A NARRATIVE: FREDERICKSBURG TO MERIDIAN.* New York: Vintage, 1986.

Holmes, Richard, Hew Strachan, Chris Bellamy, Hugh Bicheno, and Professor of the History of War and Fellow Director Oxford Program on the Changing Character of War Hew Strachan. THE OXFORD COMPANION TO MILITARY HISTORY. New York: Oxford University Press, USA, 2001.

McPherson, James M. BATTLE CRY OF FREEDOM: THE CIVIL WAR ERA. New York: Oxford University Press, 2003.

www.ingramcontent.com/pod-product-compliance
Lightning Source LLC
LaVergne TN
LVHW042000060526
838200LV00041B/1807